The Real Deal

Bullying

Joanne Mattern

Heinemann
LIBRARY

www.heinemann.co.uk/library
Visit our website to find out more information about Heinemann Library books.

To order:
 Phone 44 (0) 1865 888066
 Send a fax to 44 (0) 1865 314091
Visit the Raintree bookshop at www.heinemann.co.uk/library to browse our catalogue and order online.

Heinemann Library is an imprint of **Pearson Education Limited**, a company incorporated in England and Wales having its registered office at Edinburgh Gate, Harlow, Essex, CM20 2JE – Registered company number: 00872828

Heinemann is a registered trademark of Pearson Education Ltd.

Text © Pearson Education Limited 2009
First published in hardback in 2009
The moral rights of the proprietor have been asserted.

Edited by Kristen Truhlar, Rachel Howells, and Louise Galpine
Designed by Richard Parker and Manhattan Design
Picture research by Mica Brancic
Production: Victoria Fitzgerald

Originated by Chroma Graphics (Overseas) Pte. Ltd
Printed and bound in China by Leo Paper Group.

ISBN 978 0 431 90804 5 (hardback)
13 12 11 10 09
10 9 8 7 6 5 4 3 2 1

British Library Cataloguing in Publication Data
Mattern, Joanne, 1963-
Bullying. - (The real deal)
155.9'2

A full catalogue record for this book is available from the British Library.

Acknowledgements
We would like to thank the following for permission to reproduce photographs: ©Alamy pp. **10** (Design pics/ Kelly Redinger), **11** (Vario Images), **17** (Adrian Sherratt), **23** (David Levenson), **4, 22**; ©Corbis pp. **6** (Martin Ruetschi/Keystone), **19** (Anthony Redpath), **16**; ©Getty Images pp. **5** (Kevin Fitzgerald), **12, 21, 25** (Stone), **26** (Asia Images); ©Imagestate p. **13**; ©Jupiter Images pp. **9** (BananaStock), **24** (Workbook Stock), **15**; ©Photolibrary pp. **14** (Digital Vision), **18** (Creatas), **7**; ©PunchStock pp. **8, 27** (Tetra Images), ©Retna Ltd. (USA/Retnauk/Philip Reeson) p. **20**.

Cover photograph of a fist reproduced with permission of ©iStockphoto (borisyantov); cover photograph of teenager reproduced with permission of ©iStockphoto (ivanmateev).

We would like to thank Anne E. Pezalla for her invaluable help in the preparation of this book.

Every effort has been made to contact copyright holders of any material reproduced in this book. Any omissions will be rectified in subsequent printings if notice is given to the publishers.

Disclaimer
All the Internet addresses (URLs) given in this book were valid at the time of going to press. However, due to the dynamic nature of the Internet, some addresses may have changed, or sites may have changed or ceased to exist since publication. While the author and publishers regret any inconvenience this may cause readers, no responsibility for any such changes can be accepted by either the author or the publishers. It is recommended that adults supervise children on the Internet.

Contents

Some words are printed in bold, **like this**. You can find out what they mean by looking in the glossary.

What is bullying?

Bullying is when someone hurts another person either physically or mentally. Usually bullying happens over a period of time.

Bullying and teasing

Bullying is not the same as teasing. Sometimes friends like to tease and joke around, but teasing usually doesn't last long. Although teasing can hurt another person, it is usually meant in fun. Bullying is not fun. It is meant to hurt.

Another difference between bullying and teasing is that bullying is usually obvious. Teasing is not as obvious, and it is often disguised as joking between friends. However, teasing can also be hurtful to others. Even teasing by friends can hurt if the **victim** doesn't understand why friends are treating him or her that way.

Friends sometimes tease each other, but this is not the same as bullying.

Types of bullying

Bullying can take many forms. It can be **physical** (hitting someone) or **verbal** (calling someone hurtful names). Bullying can also be **psychological** (making someone feel weak or unwanted).

Many people think bullies are big, powerful people. That is not always true. Anyone can be a bully. A bully can be a boy or a girl. A bully can even be an adult.

Anyone can be the victim of a bully. No matter who they are, victims feel powerless and scared. People who are around a victim and a bully can feel bad too. **Witnesses**, friends, and family members are all negatively affected by bullying.

Case study

Jane had a learning disability. When she began to need special help in school, her friends started calling her hurtful names. They stopped including her in their activities. Jane felt hurt, sad, and confused. She cried every day because she was so lonely. She told her mother, "It would be nice just to be included."

Bullying makes victims feel powerless and alone.

Different types of bullying

There are many different types of bullying. No matter what type it is, all bullying is hurtful.

Physical bullying

When people think of bullying, physical bullying is often the first thing that comes to mind. Physical bullying is using force against a person. This type of bullying can include hitting, punching, kicking, or pushing someone. Physical bullying doesn't have to be a fight. It can include a person shoving another person, or causing any type of physical pain, even if the attack only lasts a few minutes.

Case study

Every time Will sees Nick at school, he pushes or hits him. A few times, he tripped or pushed Nick so hard, Nick fell down. Most recently, he's started shoving Nick into the tables whenever they pass in the canteen. Now Nick is scared to go in there alone.

People who push and shove others are using physical bullying.

Threats

Making **threats** is another kind of bullying. A bully might threaten to hurt a victim. Bullies might also threaten to damage or steal victims' property, or constantly say they are going to do something horrible to their victims.

Sometimes physical bullying is combined with threats. Bullies might beat other people up if the victims don't do something for the bullies, such as completing homework or handing over money. By frightening the victims into doing something, the bullies have power over their victims.

Some bullies damage property as a way of hurting or scaring their victims.

NEWSFLASH

Studies show that more than 30 percent of teenagers are involved in bullying, either as a victim or a bully. Some studies say that up to 90 percent of middle-school pupils have been victims of bullying at one time or another.

Shouting or saying unkind things to someone is verbal bullying.

Verbal bullying

Not all bullying is physical. Bullies can also hurt people verbally, or through words.

Like physical bullying, verbal bullying can take many forms. Verbal bullying can include calling another person names, insulting them, or saying nasty things. Making fun of a person's race, appearance, skills, or anything else is also a form of verbal bullying.

Psychological bullying

Psychological bullying is not as obvious as other kinds of bullying, but it can hurt just as much. Psychological bullying uses **emotional** attacks to make victims feel like they are not as good as other people.

NEWSFLASH

Studies show that boys and girls bully in different ways. Boys are more likely to engage in physical bullying. Girls are more likely to use psychological ways to hurt others. This may be because boys are often expected or encouraged to be rough, while girls are not.

Psychological bullying includes spreading **rumours**, **excluding** victims from activities, and encouraging the victims' friends to turn against them or ignore them. The victims' friends or classmates may gang up on them and make the victims feel unwelcome.

Sometimes the bullies make it clear to their victims that they are attacking them. Other times, they go behind people's backs, spreading rumours or turning friends against the victims. Suddenly the victims are hurt and **isolated**.

What do you think?

There is an old saying: "Sticks and stones may break my bones, but words can never hurt me." Do you think this is true? Can verbal or psychological bullying hurt as much as physical bullying?

When a group talks behind someone's back or purposely excludes the person from their group, they are using psychological bullying.

Where bullying can happen

Bullying can occur anywhere. No place is safe from bullying.

At school

Most people think of school as the place bullying happens. It is true that many pupils are bullied at school. School hallways and playgrounds are common places for bullying because large numbers of pupils are there without a lot of adult supervision. Bullying can also occur in classrooms.

Bullying often occurs in school hallways. It's easy for bullies to attack their victims without an adult present to see what's going on.

In public

Bullies can also attack in public places. Victims can be targeted when they are walking down the street, waiting for the bus, or shopping.

At home

Can bullying happen at home? Yes. Brothers and sisters can bully each other. Parents can bully children. A person could also be bullied at a friend's house, if the friend is a bully.

On the phone

Bullying can even occur when the bully and the victim are not in the same place. Bullies can hurt their victims over the phone. They can say nasty things during a phone call, or **harass** their victims by playing practical jokes over the phone.

The Internet has become a new place where bullies can hurt their victims.

Online

The Internet is another place where bullies can hurt other people. Internet bullying can involve bullies sending threats, unpleasant emails, or instant messages to a victim. Bullies may also spread rumours through email or in chat rooms, post embarrassing photos of victims on the Internet, or email the photos to other students.

Any place where a bully and a victim meet is a place where bullying can happen.

Top tips

Here are four steps that can help stop Internet bullying:

1. STOP. Don't try to talk to someone who is bullying you.
2. BLOCK. Use the "block sender" feature to prevent the bully from emailing you.
3. TALK. Tell a parent, a teacher, or another adult you trust that you are being bullied online.
4. SAVE. Save any emails or instant messages you receive from the bully, or copy information posted on websites. These can be used as evidence to prove that someone is bullying you.

Bullies and victims

People bully others for many reasons.

Feeling better about themselves

Many bullies do not have a lot of **self-esteem**. When they hurt or threaten other people, they feel powerful. Bullying makes bullies feel better than their victims.

Looking for attention

Some bullies also want to get attention. Even though hurting others is wrong, and might get them in trouble, they think it is better than being ignored.

Many bullies hurt others to feel better about themselves.

Top tips

Anyone can be a bully, but here are some tips for spotting bullies:

- Bullies often cannot control their behaviour. They act before thinking.
- Bullies do not respect the rights of others.
- Bullies always have to be right or be in control.
- Bullies have to be the centre of attention.

Some bullies come from families where a lot of fighting goes on.

Bully or victim?

Some bullies are victims themselves. Sometimes a person who is picked on and bullied by others might turn around and bully someone else. Instead of feeling powerless and scared, the new bully feels powerful.

Bullies might come from families where there is a lot of fighting and shouting. People raised in this type of family learn that it is normal to be nasty to others. It's hard for bullies to see anything wrong with their behaviour when they see it modelled at home. Studies have shown that bullies are often **abused** themselves, usually by family members.

Other reasons

Finally, some bullies pick on others for no real reason. Two people may not get along, and something makes the bully cross a line and turn to **violence**. Or maybe the bully is bored and decides to pick on someone just for fun.

Who can be a victim of a bully?

Anyone can be a victim of bullying. Some victims are chosen because of their physical appearance. Victims might look different from other people. They might wear glasses or have a disability or an illness. Victims may be heavier or thinner than their **peers**, or much taller or shorter.

Other victims might not fit in with the crowd. They are not "cool", and it's easy to pick on them because they don't act or speak like everyone else. Victims might be very shy. They might be too loud. A victim might be a new pupil at school who gets off on the wrong foot and becomes the target of a bully.

Anyone can be the target of a bully.

Case study

Karen started at a new school. Things seemed to be going well, and the popular pupils were being nice to her. Then Karen found out that one of her so-called friends had posted nasty rumours about her on the Internet. Karen started avoiding the girls at school. She even pretended to be sick so she could stay at home.

A victim of bullying may feel alone and powerless.

New pupils

Some victims might be pupils who have just moved to the area. Perhaps they have an accent or don't speak English well, or they may follow different customs from those of their classmates. Because they stand out, bullies may target them. But it is wrong for bullies to pick on people just because they are different in some way.

No reason

Often there is no clear reason why someone becomes a victim. The person might become a victim if her friends suddenly turn on her, or because someone just decides he doesn't like him. Even the most popular teenagers can be targets of a bully.

Other victims

Bullying affects a lot more people than just the victim. Friends of the victim often feel helpless. They know their friend is having a hard time, but they don't know how to stop the bullying. Or they might feel angry and decide to get back at the bully, which only causes more problems.

Witnessing an attack

People who see a bully attack someone else also suffer. Witnessing an attack can make people feel helpless, even if they don't know the victim. They might want to help the victim, but they are too scared that the bully might turn on them next. These feelings can cause even more problems. Not taking action makes witnesses feel guilty for not helping the victim or telling someone else what happened.

Witnessing a bully's attack often makes people feel helpless and guilty.

Although family members can be supportive, victims are often too ashamed to tell their parents or siblings that something is wrong.

Family matters

Victims' families can also be affected and hurt by bullying. Victims might not tell their families what's going on, but their families probably know something is wrong. Parents and brothers or sisters will want to help, but they might not be sure of the best way to do so. They might not even know their children or siblings are being bullied. Feeling confused or powerless can make family members angry and scared – the same feelings the victims are experiencing.

NEWSFLASH

Watching bullies hurt other people can make the witnesses feel so bad, they might act badly themselves. They might blame the victims and say it was the victims' fault for acting or looking "wrong", for example. Or the witnesses might stop being friends with the victims. Witnesses may think the bullies won't hurt them if the bullies think they don't like the victims either.

Bullying hurts

Bullying can hurt both **emotionally** and physically. There are many ways being the victim of a bully can damage people.

Emotional changes

People who are bullied may soon lose their self-esteem. Being picked on and harassed makes people feel small. They may think that the insults and comments they hear are true and start to believe them. They may think that because someone is picking on them, they aren't as clever or good-looking as everyone else. These feelings can affect victims long after the bullying has ended.

Being bullied also makes people feel scared and **anxious**. If victims are always expecting to be pushed, shoved, **taunted**, or harassed, they will be on guard all the time. They may think danger is around every corner and be convinced that something terrible is about to happen. Instead of concentrating on what they are doing, victims are looking around and making sure that they won't be attacked. These feelings can make life very difficult and unhappy for victims.

Being bullied doesn't just hurt physically. It can also make it hard for the victim to concentrate or take part in normal activities.

Different behaviours

Bullying can make victims change their behaviour. If a boy is picked on at the bus stop, he might decide to walk home instead of taking the bus. If a girl is pushed and shoved at football practice, she might give up and leave the team. Victims will stop doing the things they like just so they can avoid the person who is bullying them.

Victims often give up activities they enjoy to avoid running into a bully.

Case study

James was always good in school, but then his marks dropped. He couldn't concentrate because he kept worrying about an older pupil who pushed him and called him names on the bus. Some days James missed the bus on purpose. His mother had to leave work to bring him home. This made his mother angry and made James feel even worse.

More effects of being bullied

Bullying can also make the victim feel alone. Victims may feel that their friends do not understand them, so they stop spending time with their friends. They may feel that they can't share what is going on with their families either. The more isolated victims feel, the more of a target they can become. The victims feel bad so they withdraw from friends and family, but the more they withdraw the worse they feel.

Physical effects

Bullying can also cause physical symptoms. Feeling nervous and unhappy all the time can make people's stomachs hurt or make them throw up. They may not be able to sleep well. Victims might also get headaches. Now the victims are not just unhappy and scared; they also feel physically awful. This turns into a bad cycle of feeling bad physically, which makes them feel worse emotionally, which then makes the physical problems worse. It isn't hard to see how damaging bullying can be!

Being bullied can cause physical problems, such as headaches or stomachaches.

Turning the tables

Some victims become bullies themselves. They get fed up of being pushed around and start pushing other people around. This might make the victims feel powerful for a little while, but it really ends up making them feel worse.

Victims are more likely to become bullies if they are around children who are younger, smaller, or easy to pick on. They can also become bullies if they move to a new school or a new town and have a chance to start over and take on a new role.

When a victim turns into a bully, he or she normally feels even worse.

NEWSFLASH

Studies have shown that being bullied can have lasting effects on a victim. Adults who were bullied as teenagers have higher levels of sadness than adults who were not bullied. Former victims also have lower self-esteem. These feelings can last long after the bullying has stopped.

Don't be a victim

Being bullied is never the victim's fault. However, there are some ways that may prevent a person from becoming the victim of a bully. There are many **strategies** for stopping a bully.

Confidence

Being **confident** can really help. Keep your head up and walk quickly, like you know where you are going. Look the bully in the eye. Don't look down or appear to be scared.

Speaking up is also a good strategy. Sometimes, just telling bullies to stop and leave you alone will discourage them and make them see that you aren't going to be pushed around.

Another way to feel confident is to find an activity you're good at. You might join a team or a club, or take lessons in a subject that interests you. Showing your talents can be a great way to make new friends and feel good about yourself.

Participating in an activity with others can help you make friends and gain confidence.

Showing emotion

Don't let bullies see they have upset you. You might ignore them or just shrug and walk away. Using your sense of humour is a good strategy. Sometimes making a joke can **distract** bullies or make them feel less angry.

Being with other people

Spending time with other people can help you feel safe and avoid situations where bullies can catch you alone. The people you spend time with don't have to be your friends. Classmates, siblings, or many other groups of people can help.

Bullies are less likely to pick on someone when he or she is among a group.

Top tip

Many teenagers gain confidence by learning to defend themselves. Taking a **self-defence** class or learning basic self-defence techniques will give you confidence. A good teacher will help pupils learn to have the confidence to avoid **confrontations** and defend themselves without using violence.

If bullying continues

If a bully doesn't stop after being warned, telling an adult is often the best thing a victim can do. However, victims often don't want to tell an adult. They might feel embarrassed or want to pretend that everything is okay. They might think that if the bully gets in trouble, the abuse might get worse.

In reality, telling an adult can stop the bullying. A parent or teacher can take much stronger action than a young person can. It can also make the victims feel better to know they have adults on their side.

It is important to tell your parents if you are being bullied. Parents can often help make the situation better, either themselves or by reaching out to others who can help.

Top tip

Bring a friend with you when you tell an adult you are being bullied. The friend can give more details and help the adult get a better picture of what is happening. A friend will also give you support.

A school counsellor is often able to help young people deal with bullies.

Speak up!

A parent is a good person to talk to about bullying. Often a parent will contact adults where the bullying is taking place. They might also talk to the bully's parents and work out a solution to the problem. If a parent can't or won't get involved, another adult family member is a good person to ask for help.

If bullying happens at school, telling a teacher, the headteacher, or a **counsellor** is a good choice. Many schools have a **zero-tolerance policy** about bullying and will take action to solve the problem. Sometimes the solution can be as simple as changing the seating arrangement in a classroom.

Case study

When Abby found out that a bully had sent an email around school that was filled with lies that would destroy Abby's **reputation**, she showed the email to her mother. Her mother became so angry that she emailed the bully and called her mother. The bullying stopped. Best of all, Abby felt powerful because she knew her mum would fight for her.

Don't give up!

If the first adult you talk to is unwilling or unable to help, keep looking until you find someone who is willing to sort things out for you. Bullying is wrong and shouldn't happen. You are not alone, and it's important to find someone who can help.

What not to do

It may seem like a good idea for you to fight back or become a bully yourself. However, this **reaction** only ends up hurting you and other people. Fighting will only make the situation worse for everyone. You can be confident without becoming violent, and there is a better way to solve the problem.

If you find confidence in yourself, you are less likely to become the victim of a bully.

What do you think?

Some communities have passed laws against bullying. Some people think laws will stop bullies from hurting others, and give victims a way to fight back. Other people think that laws will not make any difference, and that sending a bully to prison won't stop the violence. What do you think?

Stick together

Support from friends is one of the best ways to become bully-proof. Support your friends and ask them to support you. Bullies usually back down if they are faced with a crowd. Victims won't feel so alone with a friend or two to back them up when the going gets tough.

If you see someone being bullied, don't just walk away! Step in and tell the bully to stop. If that doesn't work, tell an adult straight away. Helping others will make you feel good, and it's likely to help the victim feel better too. Most importantly, the more people who stand up to a bully, the more likely he or she will back down.

Bullying is a big problem that is difficult to solve. However, people helping each other and treating each other with respect can go a long way towards making bullies think twice about being nasty.

It is important to stick together and help others.

Facts about bullying

- A young person is bullied every 7 minutes.

- Physical bullying happens more frequently among boys.

- Verbal and psychological bullying happen more often among girls.

- In a survey of 3,000 secondary school pupils it was discovered that 70 percent of children admitted to being bullies and 56 percent have experienced bullying.

- Bullying happens in all schools and more often in sixth forms than further and higher education.

- An RNIB survey shows that nearly three in five secondary school pupils and students in further and higher education say that they had been bullied at some point.

- A survey that was carried out with more than 11,000 children by NCH over four years found that girls were more likely than boys to report bullying by email and text message.

- More than 20 percent of boys and girls share their computer passwords with their friends. Sharing passwords can lead to Internet bullying.

- Bullying can lead people to feel tense, sad, or nervous. It can affect their performance in school and their relationships with their families and friends.

Glossary

abused treated cruelly or unkindly

anxious nervous and upset

confident having a strong belief in your own abilities

confrontation meeting between people who threaten or abuse each other

counsellor someone who is trained to help people with their problems

distract make someone think of something else

emotionally having to do with strong feelings

excluding leaving someone out of an activity

harass annoy or bother constantly

isolated alone

peer classmate, workmate, or person in the same age group

physical having to do with the body

psychological having to do with feelings or emotions

reaction action in response to something

reputation your character, what people think of you

rumour story about another person that is not true

self-defence ability to protect yourself

self-esteem ability to feel good about yourself

strategy way of dealing with a problem

taunted made fun of, insulted

threat warning that something bad will happen

verbal having to do with words

victim someone who is picked on or abused by another person

violence using physical force to injure or abuse someone or something

witness person who sees something happen

zero-tolerance policy rules that say a school or other organization will not put up with any form of a certain behaviour

Further resources

Bullying is a big issue that affects many people. If you are dealing with bullying, remember that you aren't alone. As well as your family and friends, there are many resources available to help you cope with bullying.

Books

Bullies, Bigmouths and So-called Friends, Jenny Alexander
(Hodder Children's Books, 2006)

Bullying: How to Deal with Taunting, Teasing, and Tormenting, Kathleen Winkler
(Enslow Publishers, 2005)

Choices and Decisions: Dealing with Bullying, Pete Sanders (Franklin Watts, 2007)

Why Do People Bully?, Adam Hibbert (Hodder Wayland, 2004)

Websites

Anti-bullying network
www.antibullying.net/youngpeople.htm
This site looks at bullying from the point of view of eight children aged ten to seventeen.

Bullying UK
www.bullying.co.uk/pupils/index.aspx
This site explores the different types of bullying and makes suggestions on how to deal with it.

Childline
www.childline.org.uk/extra/bullyingindex.asp
There are ten top tips to beat bullying and a bullying diary to help you keep track of when you are bullied. You can also read about other people's experiences of bullying and how they beat it.

Websites (continued)

NCH, the children's charity
www.stoptextbully.com/
Read the results of a survey carried out in 2005 about mobile bullying.
There's also advice you can show your parents and teachers.

Need2know
www.need2know.co.uk/beatbullying/
There's more advice on this site including some directed at bullies themselves.

Organization

Beatbullying
Rochester House
4 Belvedere Road
London
SE19 2AT
0845 338 5060
www.beatbullying.org/index.html
Beatbullying aims to reduce and prevent bullying and the effects it has
on victims in the London area.

Index